LUCKY BOY

poems by

Mark Lilley

Finishing Line Press
Georgetown, Kentucky

LUCKY BOY

for Carson and Ben

Copyright © 2020 by Mark Lilley
ISBN 978-1-64662-369-3 First Edition
All rights reserved under International and Pan-American Copyright Conventions. No part of this book may be reproduced in any manner whatsoever without written permission from the publisher, except in the case of brief quotations embodied in critical articles and reviews.

ACKNOWLEDGMENTS

I would like to thank the editors of the following journals in which these poems first appeared:

Connecticut Review: "After the Sermon"
The Louisville Review: "New Sister"
The Midwest Quarterly: "The First Time"
Naugatuck River Review: "That Other Life"
Poet Lore: "The Check," "The Choice," "The Quiet," "Intoxication," "Memory"
Poetry Midwest: "The Leaving"
Red Rock Review: "Family"
Southern Indiana Review: "When My Father Came Around"
Sow's Ear Poetry Review: "Mother and Father"
Timber Creek Review: "Traveling With My Mother"

Publisher: Leah Huete de Maines
Editor: Christen Kincaid
Cover Art: Laura Eklund
Author Photo: Carson Lilley
Cover Design: Elizabeth Maines McCleavy

Order online: www.finishinglinepress.com
also available on amazon.com

Author inquiries and mail orders:
Finishing Line Press
P. O. Box 1626
Georgetown, Kentucky 40324
U. S. A.

Table of Contents

Traveling With My Mother 1
The Choice 2
When My Father Came Around 3
Mother and Father 4
The Leaving 5
Plea, Thirty Years Late 6
The Quiet 8
After the Sermon 9
My Mother Answers the Phone 10
The Check 11
That Other Life 12
The Visit 13
Departure 14
Bulldozer 15
Memory 16
Lucky Boy 17
Intoxication 18
Lineage 19
Family 23
New Sister 24
The First Time 26
The Brown Volare 28
Home 30
The River 31
The Promise 33

Traveling With My Mother

In the summer of 1972,
my mother bought a one-way bus ticket
from Lexington, Kentucky, to Virginia Beach.
She was almost thirty, pregnant with me,
abandoned again by my father, forced to survive
on food stamps and warehouse wages,
everything she said she'd never do
bouncing around in her head like spilled marbles.
She told her sisters that she needed to feel
sand between her toes, listen to waves
slapping against the shore.
I think she needed more. I think she needed
to stand on the earth's edge and measure
that urge to swim out, perhaps fifty yards,
and float until her mind went numb,
every mistake bubbling up in her lungs,
the sunlight turning black.
Even now when we talk about those days,
her sisters remind me that she turned around,
she hitchhiked back home,
she named me for the trucker
who bought her biscuits and gravy
without asking anything in return.

The Choice

Because it must have seemed hopeless
without a man or education to lean on,
I never blamed my mother for almost
giving my little brother away.

Just as I never blamed her for struggling
with the thought of her older sister alone
in a neighborhood noisy with children,
eggs incarcerated deep inside her sister's body.

They agreed my mother would take one week
to be sure, enough to consider what lingered
after bathing him in the sink,
blotting his brows with a blue cloth,

enough to learn the cadence of his breathing
before lowering him into the makeshift crib,
turning off the night lamp, walking away.

I'll never know when the choice was made,
how much she lived and relived
until the line was blurred between
what's selfish, what's brave.

But I remember that morning my mother
made the call, her back turned to me,
my brother wrapped carefully in his crib,

and how after hanging up the phone
she walked into the kitchen, lit the stove,
asked if I wanted something to eat.

When My Father Came Around

The old van sputtered and crackled
through Cynthiana, Kentucky,
carrying my father to another job
whenever someone passed his name.
Some nights he came around to wash his brushes,
massaging fine bristles under hot water.
He would sit alone, newspaper nearby,
my mother still at the tobacco warehouse,
nobody asking for money or his name.
Some nights he turned on the game,
drank a six-pack and waited.
He never sat me down to explain
the *hit-and-run* or *suicide squeeze*.
Some nights he made a call, changed his shirt.
Before leaving he would tap his silver lighter twice,
smoke one cigarette. I watched it burn
through his fingertips into some dark cell,
hating myself for a love I had little reason to feel.

Mother and Father

When she comes home from a double shift
to his indifference, to his thoughts that may
or may not include her, she spits on him.
He doesn't answer back, even when she
gets in his face, close enough to smell
his breath, to see that he hasn't shaved in days,
to see that he hasn't smiled or frowned
since he was a child. She calls him *two-timer*
and *sonofabitch* and tells him where he's going
when he dies. And still she fries two pork chops.
And before he walks out for a month,
before he disappears without telling anyone
where he's going, he stretches out on the couch.
She takes his head in her lap and runs
her fingers through black hair,
under his T-shirt stained with paint,
the room suddenly soft, and in the softness
he strokes her arm, he finds her hand
and holds it until he falls asleep,
and she lets him sleep.

The Leaving

Take me with you, I want to say,
though I don't say the words,
even as my mother sits alone,
the radio mocking her with
My Woman, My Woman, My Wife.

I stand at the screen door—
through aluminum squares
his body seems less frail—
and watch him drive away,

off to a liquor joint or country road
missing from maps, his jalopy
spitting oil, darkening the dirt path
that leads out of our trailer park.

Plea, Thirty Years Late

Lift the chipped cup to your lips,
coffee black with a pinch of sugar.
You should be sleeping next to a man
whose stubble rouses you into waking.
But your man is holed up with Josie
in a double-wide outside Maysville.
Josie. Red-head, hippie hair.
Go ahead. Burn the photograph you found
folded in my father's wallet—
Josie's slender frame kneeling
next to the Doberman he rescued,
a birthday gift for her youngest son.
Assume Josie's unbuttoning the shirt
you washed, the shirt you pressed
and hung on the shower rod.
Assume my father will never marry you.
Assume his name is too good
for the girl from Fern Creek,
the girl who walked home on railroad tracks
after long days stripping tobacco.
Assume he was nothing more
than a way out of the valley, a promise
you made to your momma on the porch.
Recall your momma's hair, black as soot,
the homemade pajamas she sewed
from cot linens. Recall the hymns she sang
as you chased fireflies deep into the hollow.
Go ahead. Picture my father stranded on Highway 27.
Picture him startled by the scarcity of stars,
coyotes yipping in the uncertain distance.
Picture him in the dark calling out Josie's name.
Go ahead. Aunt Connie will buy
our bus tickets to Pensacola.
We will convert the shed behind
her house, share a common yard.

I will make new friends, find a team
that needs an all-star shortstop.
Go change out of your drab nightgown.
Before you grease the skillet.
Before you fiddle with the radio knob.
Before he gets sick and Josie kicks him out.
Mother, the front door is waiting. Go ahead.
I will forgive you.

The Quiet

I sit up in bed again long past midnight,
my little brother asleep beside me.
I am ten years old. I hear through the vents
my mother talking to my father.
They are in bed together. She's reminding him
of the cancer that has spread to his brain.
She asks gently—trying not to pressure him—
if he will marry her, if he will go tomorrow
to the county courthouse and sign the papers.
She wants him to think of his boys, to imagine
what it would mean for us to own his name.
During the quiet my brother turns
his slender body to mine. Before he wakes
and asks me if everything is okay,
I hear my mother moving between rooms.
She is cleaning, straightening,
pulling something out, putting something away.

After the Sermon

The pastor and his family piled
into their station wagon.
I remember the chrome headlights,
his wife adjusting the youngest girl's bow,
laughter and singing spilling out
as if the engine turning
were reason enough to praise God.
As the congregation dwindled,
my mother began cleaning the pews,
her brown shirt blending with the wood.
My job was to follow behind, straighten up
if something seemed out of place.
In the quiet of United Methodist,
she mopped the floor with bleach and water,
dusted candelabras, polished offering plates
until our reflection appeared in the gold center.
Before turning out the lights, she stood
behind the pulpit as if she wanted to speak,
as if an audience anticipated her words.
Then we gathered our supplies, loaded the Volare.
I watched her lock the church doors
and finish one cigarette, puffs of smoke
dissolving above us like prayers.

My Mother Answers the Phone

I squat between the washer and dryer,
not exactly hiding, not exactly praying,
fingers crossed that my father hasn't killed himself.

Before walking out without his wallet
and silver lighter, he said he would rather
disappear forever than go back to the V.A. Hospital.

What does it mean that my mother's shadow
has stopped pacing?

Everything might be okay. Or everything
might sting like my father's hooch,
like the sip he encouraged me to take
on the front porch in broad daylight.

I'm only ten, too young to know
why men drift, where they linger,
what happens when a woman receives word.

The Check

After my father died, we survived
on a monthly social security check.

My mother would remind me
the check needed to stretch an entire month,

which was possible before
her younger sister called asking for money.

She was always alone and between jobs,
promising not to buy drugs or liquor

or take up with a man twice her age,
and sometimes my mother said *No*

or something softer like *Let me see, Priscilla*
before hanging up,

returning to her coffee and envelopes,
making a list.

That Other Life

At twelve I became hooked
on my mother's favorite soap opera,
rushing home after school to catch
the second half of *Days of Our Lives*.

During those long summer days
when boys my age were playing baseball,
I remained in front of the television,
rooting for romance and second chances.

When Bo's car plunged over a cliff
I could barely watch as Hope received the news
in her wedding dress, unleashing a grief
that convinced me the pain was real.

Bo wasn't really dead, of course, and the removal
of his bandages revealed a different actor
with darker hair. I cried when this new Bo
kissed her fingertips and cupped her face,

those violins reminding me of my mother
smoking alone in the dark, never receiving
the heartfelt phone call that sent her out
into the rainy night, into the arms

of my father who always disappeared
without taking a change of clothes, whose secrets
were merely something they might have laughed about
or dismissed as what happened in that other life.

The Visit

It's just another Saturday visit
when the social worker tells my mother
time is running out, and the broken windows
must be replaced or my brother and I
will be removed from the home.
She says the state won't allow us to live
this way, the worst of winter still to come,
and surely there must be someone
willing to take us in.

My mother joins us on the plaid-splattered couch,
the walls as dim as her nightgown.
She pulls an old cigarette from the ashtray,
holding her match steady until the stub glows.

Departure

Two hours before departure,
our new stepfather finds an airport bar
while we wait with our mother at the gate.

She tells us sometimes he needs to escape
the stress of this life, the pressure
of finding and keeping work, of providing.

But we shouldn't worry because she understands him
the way Mildred, his first wife, never could,
and men need to be understood or else

their stinginess might be mistaken for secrets,
which leads to accusations,
which leads to something broken.

We should feel grateful that she found a man
who would marry her, who vowed
to remain faithful night and day.

She wants us to know we're a team now,
four soldiers marching in the same direction,
only as strong as our weakest link.

Bulldozer
for Scott

I remember the field across our street
before the bulldozer plowed through,

where in the summer of 1985
my brother and I would run and hide

and wait for our stepfather to pass out,
where each day at dusk a small possum—

leg lame, patches of fur missing—
would find us crouched in the tall grass.

We were careful not to startle it.
Back then everything was startling enough,

our stepfather drunk and dangerous,
warning us to never bring home a dog

or cat or hamster, no living things
for us to nurse or bathe or feed.

So we would leave behind bread crumbs
and plastic ashtrays filled with water.

If we'd been like the Nickerson twins
we might have strangled the possum

and paraded it around our trailer park.
But we were not hateful or cruel,

and when the bulldozer came that summer day
we ran out of the field barefoot,

covered in chiggers, waving our arms
until the man in a hardhat high atop

the claw machine stopped and listened—
Please, give us five minutes, please.

Memory

When I was twelve, I watched my stepfather
pistol-whip a raccoon that was eating his tomatoes.

That summer I learned many words: *carcass,
fermentation, Alpha Charlie, cocksucker.*

It was the same gun he lodged under the front seat
on our weekend trips to Atlanta when we'd visit

his mother. We mostly sat around as nurses
changed her bedpan or flushed her feeding tube.

Once, she started talking in her sleep about running
barefoot through woods until she came to a river.

I thought it was another dream of the dying.
But on the drive home my stepfather told me

about that Easter morning when he was twelve,
how they were awakened by the sound

of his father's hunting dog scratching
at the screen door, and how he followed his mother

through patches of clover and foamflower,
and what they found downstream.

Lucky Boy
>*for Mr. S*

He never put his mouth on me
the way another man might have
if he had found himself alone with a boy
whose mother worked weekends.

He never got me hard with a magazine
pulled from his glove compartment
as we drove to Cincinnati and back
in a sedan whose windows were not tinted.

He never took me behind a rest stop
where the undergrowth was thick,
and rigs hauling turbines on I-75
might have drowned out a boy's squeal.

He never seduced me with jerseys
or bobbleheads. He never told a joke
that needed to stay between us.
He never asked about my dead father

until what I desired—even more
than a late inning rally—
was to rest my head on a man's shoulder,
to feel his three-day-old stubble.

That summer I was a lucky boy. He was just
a 7th grade science teacher who shared my love
of baseball, who dropped me off with nothing
but a scorecard folded in my pocket.

Intoxication

During jury selection the lawyer asked
if I understood the word *intoxication*.
I remembered one summer at a country lake,
my mother and father in drab suits
trying to forget what they had done to each other.
They sat at the end of the dock. He held a Strohs
in one hand, his other arm dangled
over her shoulder like a broken hinge.
She tossed her head back as he kissed her neck.
He was finding words. He called her *baby*.
No one could make the blue sky go away.
Even as he struggled to his feet,
even as she held him steady
so he wouldn't fall over the edge,
no one could judge what remained—
sunburned skin, wrinkled water,
two shadows trying to become one.

Lineage

      1.

Because I wanted him to know the man
in the grainy photograph,
I brought my son to see
where his grandfather rested.

It was here that a flag unfurled
and I counted stars and stripes
until the numbers added up to sorrow.
My son was not much taller

than the three-foot tombstone,
and with nothing to say
and no trumpets announcing my sorrow
I turned us away from the old story.

We crossed over to a hillside without graves,
without a church and its broken bell,
and it was here that I counted twenty-three shrubs
before my son said *Dad*

and ran down where the creek thinned,
where the wildflowers bloomed blue-green.
By the time I caught up,
he was ankle-deep in the shallows,

and it was here in the dead of summer
that my son counted twelve tadpoles,
sweet boy without memory,
sweet boy who'd buried no one.

      2.

If you lived at the top of Antioch Hill
you could have watched the beginning and end
of my father's story—
log cabin where he was born

during The Great Depression, the schoolhouse
where he learned to add and subtract
and to write the name he refused my mother,
Berry Methodist where he never married,

and next to the church
the graveyard with its embedded stones,
where under a tilted canopy in the rain
we buried him, our tired stranger.

    3.
My father was at the recruiting office
when word came that his father
had fallen from a scaffold
while painting the drive-in marquee.

Two days later my father buried his father
and boarded a bus to Baton Rouge,
the Army indifferent to his grief.
He was seventeen.

    4.
Another story was told. I can't repeat it.
The man who told me served
in the Army with my father.
It was a story with two dawns, two dusks.

On the first day, work you do to prepare—
loading knapsacks, filling canteens,
cleaning the lens of a rifle's scope,
sitting down to write a letter.

On the second day, quiet.
Except for something launched, and the sound
the ground makes after something's launched.
I can't repeat it, but my father survived.

5.
One morning I rode with my father
to the V.A. Hospital. He had stopped drinking
and thought the headaches
were God's punishment for his waiting so long.

He waved at truckers, said they reminded him
of driving for Schneider, delivering turbines
to factories in Topeka and Des Moines,
factories, my father said, where men made light.

Safe memory, go on—with one hand
my father pulls a cigarette
from his shirt pocket,
and with the same hand lights up,

and the small fire at the tip glows
against the peach horizon, and I am ten and shy,
but I say the words *peach horizon,*
and my father looks west.

6.
My son wants to hear a new story.
Okay, a new story: A boy runs away
and is forgiven. That boy becomes a bigger boy
and watches his friends wring a cat's neck,

and the boys in the trailer park are forgiven,
and years later the boy becomes a man
who falls in love with the right woman
at the wrong time, and the man is forgiven,

and the fruit bowl is glued back together,
all seventeen pieces, and this is the story
in which you salvage something broken,

something dropped or slung

in your direction, and *why*
is not important in the new story,
sweet boy drifting in his cotton pajamas,
sweet boy who's betrayed no one.

Family

This afternoon I imagine my dead father
picking up his granddaughter from school.
She is unashamed of the rusted van.
The front seat is wider than regret.
The windows are rolled up,
radio playing George Jones.
He struggles to ask about her day,
the other children, how her favorite bow
came undone mid-afternoon.
He notices her hair, black as a chalkboard,
the dimples in her cheeks, the long blink
before her eyes meet his. She is ten
and feels the weight of his sadness.
He fiddles—as he does when he's nervous—
with his painter's cap. He's longing
for a cup of coffee, a cigarette, something to eat.
She tells him a story about riding her bike
through slippery leaves. He listens
before coughing a stale cough, as if clearing
his throat for the words that will not follow.

New Sister

When I receive the phone call from a woman
in Iowa who claims she's my half-sister,

who says the DNA kit she ordered online
confirmed with 99.94% certainty

we share the same father, I laugh.
Not because I don't believe her story,

and not because the first thing she said
after I said Hello was, *I bet your voice*

sounds just like our daddy's did,
but because it strikes me as funny—

maybe for the first time—to imagine
my father driving his rig into those sad towns,

always on the prowl for some sad woman.
He must have found one wherever he drifted—

truck-stop diners, roadhouses with beat-up jukeboxes,
laundromats where he could charm single mothers.

I want to tell my new sister
that our father drank too much,

that he lied about where his paycheck went,
that he refused to marry my mother

even after he got cancer and there was nothing
doctors could do, even after his favorite girlfriend

kicked him out and my mother took him back
into her bed, even after she pressed

the cold rags to his forehead
and emptied his jars of phlegm.

But when my new sister tells me her story—
how she was abandoned at birth,

how her adoptive parents unleashed
their Catholic punishment,

how she's never trusted any man,
and how it might mean everything

to hear one sweet memory, proof
that she inherited something decent,

some light she might carry through the darkness,
her plea deteriorating into tears

and then a sobbing that frightens me,
I decide to pull back.

I tell my new sister about that morning
riding shotgun with our father,

how on the way to the V.A. Hospital
he picked up a hitchhiker,

a fellow whose head was shaved,
whose scar wrapped from ear

to ear, and our father asked this fellow
how he was getting along.

The First Time

The older boys swear it's true.
They have been there before,
have seen men coming and going.
So we pile in the back of my cousin's pickup
and ride out to Highway 27, past the roller rink
and Joe Tully's tobacco farm, beyond
the juice joints and card shacks,
out where the darkness swells but hides nothing.

We drive over Ogden Bridge where last summer
the Nickerson twins jumped into the Licking River,
holding hands, the story goes,
when divers found their bodies tangled
in fishing wire. Someone says their names—
Tommy and Ray— and the boys are with us again,
ghosts on the faint tips of treetops.

On Antioch Road pavement turns to gravel.
Stars wobble. Rocks spit out from under the tires,
startling night critters nestled in the brambles.
Through a clearing we see the cockeyed trailer.
We park in the dirt, walk up concrete blocks
and peer in the lone window.

On the edge of an unmade bed
she sits in a red nightgown, braless.
I notice the soft droop of her breasts,
the bony outline of her shoulders, charcoal hair
pinned and glossy, and for the first time
I think of sadness and beauty as one

because a baby is sleeping in a plastic crib,
a baby wearing pink socks, the shadow
of a candle flame on her belly,
and our giddiness subsides
until there is nothing but quiet.

As new headlights emerge in the distance,
we turn away from the window,
careful not to wake her.

The Brown Volare

On the road to my high-school reunion,
I spot a brown Volare, and with time to spare

I decide to follow its dented fender
through my hometown.

I pass the gravel lot of Ronnie's Drive-In,
the big screen advertising legal advice.

I follow the rusted chrome, doors peeling,
as it veers onto Elmarch Avenue,

the street lined with government duplexes,
single mothers smoking on shared porches.

I follow its tail of exhaust to Highway 27
where hay bales are rolled like fists.

I follow its groan uphill towards Cassie's house,
surprised when it pulls into her driveway

and a boy steps out who must be sixteen,
his collared shirt tucked into dark jeans.

I follow his thin, untouched body
to the front door, waiting as he waits,

our hearts pounding, our fingers fidgeting
with car keys, and when the screen door opens

I follow his hand until it finds hers,
and I think of those boys loading dye

at Bundy Tubing, boys stripping tobacco
in the county warehouse, and this boy

swallowed up in the front seat,
the engine turning on a prayer.

Home

At dusk I'm walking with my father
from the general store to Boodle's Tavern,
holding his hand as the sun slips
behind factory towers. Farther away
a howling rattles the hills. I believe him
when he says the howling will die out
before dawn, before my mother lights a stove
and disappears into tobacco fields.
He needs a drink and tells me to wait
in the gravel lot. Beyond the brush
the Licking River runs slick and silky.
Men come and go.
They wear ball caps and look down.
I imagine them as boys and feel a boy's ache.
Because the river is something to fear,
and the brush will scrape their arms,
and I know my father is alive
only in the living sense.
Nothing is left that can break his heart.

The River

This morning you find me murky and swollen
after overnight rains. I rose two feet
and flooded the ball fields on River Road.
Forgive me. Forgive the storm front that started
over the plains and swept eastward, jolting
small children from slumber.
While you were driving I drudged along
past refineries and junkyards,
through the stench of cured tobacco.
Forgive my persistence. I prefer not knowing
what lingers in the dark, the mysterious rustling
between trees, footsteps and whispers
without shape, without faces,
never far from my swerving.
What I know is that he parked his van
near the shallow end, where the quarry rubs
against the flood wall.
He turned off the ignition, but not right away.
I've seen this before, middle-aged fathers at my edge.
I don't know why they seek me out,
what tugs them towards my dank glow.
He removed his painter's cap.
A flurry of blackbirds burst from the trees.
I can't be sure if he watched them divide,
but he rolled down his window
and leaned into fresh air, into light
that fell jagged across vinyl seats.
I thought he might join me.
I've seen it before. Sometimes they enter
as if taking a stroll in the park,
as if meeting an old friend for coffee,
until their legs buckle and for an instant
I believe they're ready to fight me.

But more often they submit, sinking
below my brown sheen until they emerge
with the same sadness, the same misery
they were certain would be washed away
by one gesture selfish and brave.
I could go on with these stories,
but you want to know what happened
before a fisherman found him the next day,
his wrist scabbed and bloated,
still alive because he wanted to live.
I can tell you he was a handsome man,
slender jawbone, jaunty hair slicked back,
eyes wide and hazel like yours,
and there was a gentleness about him,
the way he rested his head against the seat.
It's not difficult imagining him cupping
the face of a good woman, and with one finger
removing a stray hair from her forehead.
Maybe you choose to remember him like this.
Maybe you recall a night in a trailer
when the air was soft and clean,
and no one was afraid.
I wish I could give you more
because you've traveled so far to be here.
It's a lonely drive home through the valley.
Forgive me. The wind has shifted again,
hinting at what's to come.

The Promise

In the dream my father is chopping wood.

He inspects for knots and knuckles
before splitting each log along the grain.

I push the wheelbarrow to a dead patch
near the winter shed. Because I'm a boy

who knows that a pile of wood needs to breathe,
I stack the halves crossways.

My mother is stirring something on the stove.

Chores complete, my father and I sit together
on the back stoop.

Smoke rises from the burn barrel.

He promises to take me fishing at sunrise
when river trout are feeding in the cool shallows.

Additional Acknowledgements

I am grateful to my Butler MFA classmates, especially to Tracy Mishkin for her thoughtful reading; to Chris Forhan who went above and beyond with the attention he gave these poems; to George Eklund for his early encouragement and influence; to William Caywood, and to all of the teachers, and to Lori Lilley for her unwavering support.

Special thanks to Alessandra Lynch for her gifts as a poet, as a professor, and as a human being.

Mark Lilley was born and raised in Cynthiana, Kentucky. He earned his undergraduate degree from Morehead State University and his MFA in poetry from Butler University. His poems have appeared in *Connecticut Review, The Louisville Review, The Midwest Quarterly, Naugatuck River Review, Poet Lore, Plainsongs, Sow's Ear Poetry Review, Southern Indiana Review,* and other journals. Between poems he works in a leadership position for a mutual fund service company. He currently lives in Fishers, Indiana, with his wife and two children.